© Paul Gaskell and John Pearson 2020

All rights reserved. This book or parts thereof may not be reproduced in any form, stored in any retrieval system, or transmitted in any form by any means—electronic, mechanical, photocopy, recording, or otherwise—without prior written permission of the publisher, except as provided by United States of America and/or international copyright law. For permission requests, write to the publisher, at "Attention: Permissions Coordinator," at the address below:

Paul Gaskell

paul@fishingdiscoveries.com

Website: www.fishingdiscoveries.com

Please consider leaving a review for this book on Amazon - it helps to ensure we can continue publishing new content

Thank you!

Contents

Introducing Pocket Guidance to Increasing your Success when Fly Fishing Small Streams — 4

A Small Stream Fly Fishing Manifesto — 5

Safe Bet Flies for Small Streams — 7
Important Notes on Flies — 15

Fundamental Tactics & Skills — 17
Reading water — 17

Single Dry Fly — 19

Duo/Hopper-Dropper — 20

Double and Single Nymph or Wet Fly — 21

Streamer Fishing — 22

   Tactics: Key Components — 24

Top 10 Tips: #1. Use the LONGEST Rod Possible — 25

2. Use "Hand-lining" Under Low Canopy — 27

3. Catapult or Slingshot Cast — 30

4. Roll Cast — 31

5. Side-cast under canopy — 32

6. Choose a Specialist Casting Line or Leader	35
7. Use Currents to Fish "Impossible" Spots	36
8. Fish Downstream More Often than you Might Think	38
9. In Tight Streams - Pick a Direction and Work it	39
10. Two Anglers to a Rod	42
Researching & Finding New Small Streams to Fish	43
Rules of Engagement:	43
Suggested Tools	43
Google Maps' "Special Features"	44
What does slope tell you anyway?	47
Google Satellite View	48
Underlying Geology (BGS and USGS)	49
Open Signal	51
Magic (GIS) - UK only	52
Onstream Video & E-books of Small Stream Maestro #1: Kazunori Kobayashi	53
Re-discover "Lost" Tactics of Small Stream Maestro #2: Henry Charles Cutcliffe	54
Small Streams Fishing Trip Log	55

Introducing Pocket Guidance to Increasing your Success when Fly Fishing Small Streams

*"In fly fishing, your success is mostly down to **not screwing up** before the fish has seen your fly"*

That's not the way that most anglers see the challenge though...

Instead, there is a persistent idea that you need to create the perfect artificial fly, deliver it with a pure, dead-drift presentation and keep everything crossed that your insect identification has not embarrassed you in front of the trout.

In reality, the two most important factors are probably whether you can get your fly in front of the fish - while not scaring it to death in the process.

The quickfire tactics in this guide are all methods that we've used to give ourselves and our guiding clients a significant edge (and show the value of not really following the herd).

Inside, you'll find a proven Small-Streams fly collection, guidance on reading the water - plus secrets of using online data sources to discover new small trout streams to fish. We also give you 10 ways to help you to avoid splashing, spooking, tangling, missing the target or otherwise blowing your chances. It's the pocket guide to big results I wished I had when I got started on my addiction to casting flies at trout in little rivers.

My assumptions, before you read this book, are that you can fly cast, attach a fly to tippet and either tie or order custom flies.

If you enjoy the success we've planned for you with the tactics in this guide, then make sure to double down and continue absorbing our masterclass material here:

https://doublebadgers.kartra.com/page/smallstreams35

A Small Stream Fly Fishing Manifesto

There is an obvious, grand appeal to a large and majestic trout river. It could be a gliding, serene lowland reach or a thundering, swirling deadly torrent. Either way it is difficult to avoid being impressed.

For a select number of anglers, though, there is a very special attraction to the small, sometimes hidden and always intimate nature of a little trout stream. Leading figures such as John Gierach are hooked on the strange delights of "sneaking round on your hands and knees". In fact, anyone familiar with Gierach's writing will know about his love affair with the little St. Vrain river (which he points out is more accurately described on some maps as the St. Vrain Creek).

Beautiful, wild and vibrant. If you only judge trout (and trout streams!) on how big they are, then I believe you're missing a trick.

Perhaps you are addicted to following that faint blue map line of a headwater stream ever-higher towards the mountain-top? Maybe you love to discover trickles among overgrown tangles in the woods? You might even spend your time rediscovering little forgotten tributaries that are home to urban trout.

Whatever the case, this little guide can help set you up to create some great memories on-stream. There's tactics, "Top-10" tips, flies and tutorials to increase your chances of success, save a blank day or simply reduce frustration on these tricky, tactical waters with so much character. *Let's begin with flies...*

Sneaking away with a rod to fish a simple fly under the trees in a hidden corner; ingredients for magic!

Safe Bet Flies for Small Streams

Let's get one thing straight - the **wrong fly with the right presentation still has a fair chance of success**. That's because the first box any "right presentation" needs to check is the one for "not scaring the fish".

However, the right fly with the wrong presentation has almost zero chance of success. Maybe it puts your fly in the wrong place (where the fish can't see it). Perhaps it moves the fly in a way that repels fish. Worst of all, a bad presentation could spook the fish before it has even seen the fly.

Accepting that presentation comes first, it still inspires confidence to have a solid and proven set of fly patterns. It basically means there's one less thing to worry about. That's why I've opened up my box of a small selection of patterns which deliver the goods for me on small streams all around the world. It covers the most important pillars of what's likely to be on the menu for game fish in little rivers, namely:

Adult caddis (big and small) are covered by two patterns tested to destruction by competition anglers - A "Retirer Sedge" variant (original pattern by Davie Parker) and "Competition Caddis" variants I believe started life in Poland.

Adult midges (dry and drowned) as well as emerging, drowned or adult small mayflies/olives are covered by the ever-adaptable Ishigaki-style kebari. Fussy, flat-water olive-feeding fish can also be shown a slim CDC olive dun.

Caddis and midge larvae/pupae have JP's "Easy bugs" to take care of them. Also my mobile-hackle option for caddis pupae - plus a reliable scud/freshwater shrimp for calcareous streams.

Straight-bodied nymphs like stoneflies and olives are covered by the tailed/bead-head patterns from tiny sizes and upwards - including a "post egg-laying" baetis spinner.

Finally, streamers for targeting those small-stream carnivores!

Retirer Sedge Variant
Sizes 14 - 10

Hook: Fish On Nymph/Wet
Body: Brown Fish On NBC dubbing
Underwing: Fish On Ultra Dry Yarn
(sulphur yellow or light orange)
Overwing: Deer Hair (dyed olive)
Head: Brown/grey dubbing mix

Competition Caddis (Cul-de-Canard/"CDC" wing
& extended, furled body)
Sizes 18-12

Hook: Barbless dry fly of your choice
Thorax: Grey squirrel
Abdomen: Finger-Twisted & doubled loop of yarn or long-fibre dubbing (orange or pink)
Wing: 2 or 3 CDC feather tips

Grey or Olive "Tailed" Ishigaki (for wet or dry)
Sizes 16 - 10

Hook: Your choice of dry fly hook e.g. Fish On Dry Fly
Body: Sewing Thread roughly wrapped to make ribbed segments
Collar Hackle: Badger Cock - roughly lash back stray fibres to make tail

Black Ishigaki Variant (wet or dry)
Sizes 21- 12

Hook: Fine wire for dry medium or thick wire for wet (curved or straight)
Body: Black Sewing Thread touching turns
Hackle: Grizzle or Ginger Cock - tied with underside facing eye of hook

CDC Olive Dun
Sizes 22- 16

Hook: Barbless dry fly of your choice
Body: Hends Body Quills in Olive
Wing: 1 or 2 CDC feather tips
Tail: 3 "micro-fibbets" from a watercolour paintbrush

Bead-head CDC Baetis Spinner
Sizes 18 - 14

Hook: Straight-shank barbless nymph/wet e.g. Knapek or Fish On
Body Front 2/3rds: Hends Body Quills in Brown
Body Rear Third: Hends Body Quills in Orange
"Hackle": CDC fibres in dubbing loop
Tail: Clump of watercolour paintbrush micro-fibbets
Stub wing: Pearly tinsel dubbing (pinch and then clipped)
Head: Tungsten bead (copper or silver)

Straight-bodied Nymph
Sizes 20- 8

Hook: Fish On Nymph/Wet or similar nymph hook
Body: Olive or Brown UTC Wire in open Turns
Underbody: Tying silk (either brown or yellow)
Thorax: Grey Squirrel, dubbed and brushed out
Tails: Micro fibbets or Coq-de-Lyon or hackle barbs
Head: Tungsten bead in white, lime green or orange

Little Olive
Sizes 22- 18

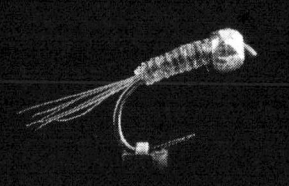

Hook: Tiemco BL103 or 100 SPBL
Body: Olive Fish On Ultimate Body Rib (Fine)
Tails: Hackle barbs or extra fine micro fibbets
Head: 1.5-mm Tungsten bead (copper or natural metal)

JP Easy Bug in Grey Sparkle
Sizes 16 - 8

Hook: Curved/grub (e.g. Fish On Curved)
Body: Pale Grey Fish On NBC Dubbing - with optional brushed-out collar hackle of same
Rib: Silver Wire (Medium)
Head: Silver Tungsten Bead - matched to hook-size

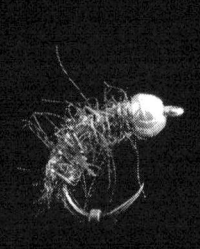

Easy Bug Variants
Sizes 20- 10

Hook: Curved/grub or Jig
Body: Black seal's fur or sub - with optional brushed-out collar hackle of same
Rib: Red Wire (Fine or Medium)
Head: Tungsten Bead - pink anodised or natural metal

Natural Minkie Streamer
Sizes 12 - 8

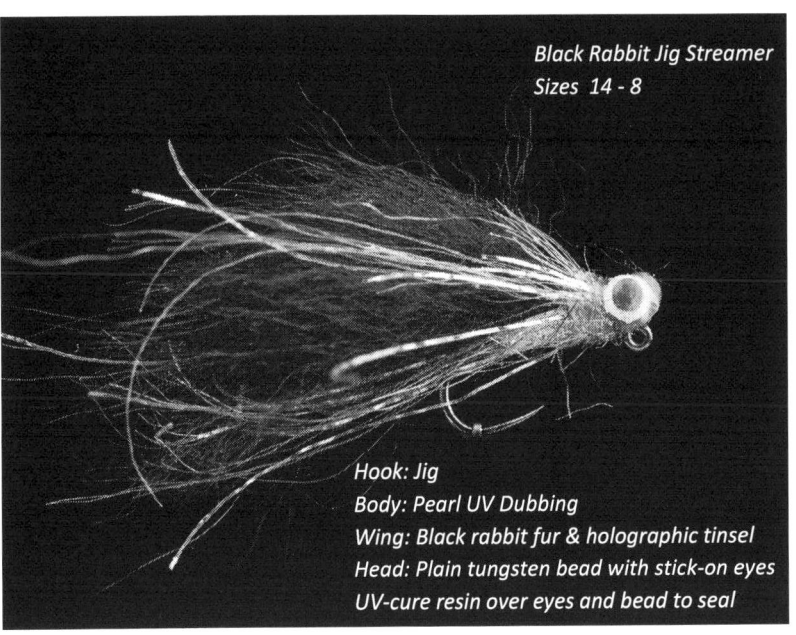

Hook: Streamer, long-shank
Body: Pale cream dubbing with holographic tinsel lashed alongside
Rib: Silver Wire (wound over holographic tinsel and through wing-fibres)
Wing: Natural mink strip
Head: Brown dubbing with stick-on 3-D eyes glued each side
Bead: Hot orange Tungsten bead to suit hook/required sink-rate

Black Rabbit Jig Streamer
Sizes 14 - 8

Hook: Jig
Body: Pearl UV Dubbing
Wing: Black rabbit fur & holographic tinsel
Head: Plain tungsten bead with stick-on eyes
UV-cure resin over eyes and bead to seal

PG Hackled Caddis Pupa or "Pharate Adult"
Sizes 16-12

Hook: Curved Grub
Body: Pale Cream synthetic dubbing (turns translucent when wet)
Underbody: Touching turns of chartreuse rib material
Rib: Chartreuse UTC Ultra wire
Hackle: Grey partridge
Head: Tungsten bead in silver or copper

PG Sight Spider Variant
Sizes 16-12

Hook: Nymph/wet
Body: Black Flyrite
Hackle: White Hen (reverse or normal orientation)
Head: White tying thread

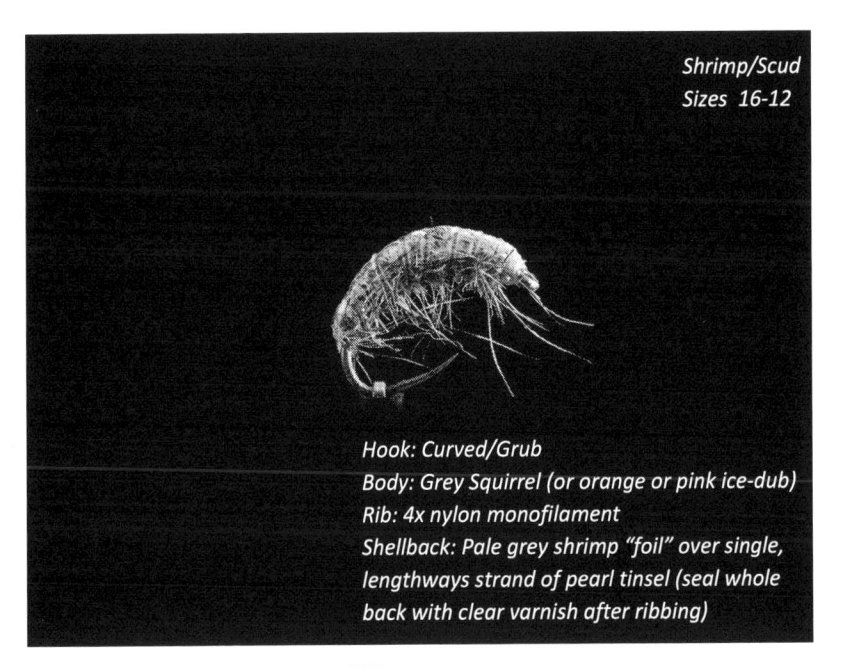

> *Shrimp/Scud*
> *Sizes 16-12*
>
> *Hook: Curved/Grub*
> *Body: Grey Squirrel (or orange or pink ice-dub)*
> *Rib: 4x nylon monofilament*
> *Shellback: Pale grey shrimp "foil" over single, lengthways strand of pearl tinsel (seal whole back with clear varnish after ribbing)*

Important Notes on Flies

There's one thing I need to stress about flies in general - and particularly this collection here:

Adapt them to your own needs - and don't be too hung up on specific materials

I've included material listings or **suggestions to get you started**, but feel free to substitute according to what's available to you. The fly collection is designed to be an "all-purpose, go-anywhere" squad that you can draw on and modify. As we'll see in the tactics section, the Retirer sedge can act either as a dry fly in it's own right - or as the floating fly in a "duo"/"hopper-dropper" rig. Think of all the flies in the same way - and be creative in the FUNCTIONS that you give to each fly.

Some particular tactical notes are useful for the more unusual patterns (over the page). I should also offer an explanation of *calcareous* as to its significance to shrimps and scuds.

In streams with base-rich water (e.g. limestone or chalk streams), lush plant-growth is coupled with a ready supply of the calcium needed to make strong shells for crustaceans. Result: tons of shrimp/scuds. Using both drab (including olive-dyed squirrel dubbing versions) and the super-bright options can be essential to trigger fish on different days.

The "Sight Spider" style of dressing is a great way of introducing stealth on streams with spooky fish. Sometimes having anything other than a single fly causes the fish to bolt. By making the hackle visible to the angler (but not a scary colour to the fish) allows you to deliver a single fly, sub-surface which acts as its own strike indicator. This also removes the need for a potentially scary conventional strike indicator further up the tippet or line.

Females (i.e. egg-laying individuals!) of *Baetis* species crawl down rocks (or branches or bridge-supports) below the surface of the water to lay their eggs underneath stones on the stream bed. When they finish that task, they just let go and drift off downstream. This is precisely what the bead-head egg-laying spinner imitates. It also explains the inclusion of the sparkle in the wing - since spinners have much glossier wings than duns.

The variations on the Ishigaki theme are a great example of something evident across all the flies in this selection: Don't be afraid to dress **scruffy & mobile** or **neat & tidy** depending on the effect you need. Where mobility and the impression of life are important, tying fast and creating chaotic outlines are important - so *have the confidence to tie that way* when you need to. For flat, low water (and "low background noise") or where you need a fly to cut cleanly through the water, *tie neatly and go for slim profiles*. For the Ishigaki specifically, remember to match the hook-wire to whether you want to a dry fly or a wet fly. Also be happy to use rough, open/criss-crossing turns of thick thread to create a segmented body.

Finally, chartreuse wire under *see-through-when-wet* dubbing creates an awesome imitation of hatching caddis abdomens. Marrying that with a kicking legs hackle is a dynamite combo...

Fundamental Tactics & Skills

I've already mentioned being creative with the functional roles of your flies. A prime example of that is to choose the sink-rate of your tail fly (or point fly) to pull down a slower-sinking or much smaller dropper fly. However, because I could talk all day about that sort of thing, I need to focus on more fundamental skills for this pocket guide.

Reading water

Again, this is a subject that should fill several books. That being said, the close-quarters fishing on little streams - and the concentration of features into small areas - is a great way to increase your water-reading skills.

What you learn on small streams is then a fantastic guide to where you will find fish on larger rivers. The same features can just occur at larger scales (or sometimes at exactly the same scale - but surrounded by a LOT more water).

Key factors to look out for are:

- Route of food supply & concentration (i.e. currents)
- Cover from other predators nearby
- Less need to fight the current while waiting for food to arrive

The fastest way to get good at this is to ask yourself two questions:

1. *Where is the food coming from - and where is it carried?*

2. *Where are the boundaries between contrasting conditions?*

The first one is straight forward - but not always easy to see. A great guide is to track the trail of bubbles flowing downstream. The more concentrated a foam highway, the more food is likely to be being carried by that "conveyer belt". You should also look out for where the food might originate. Riffles are a plentiful and diverse source of food - particularly in warmer months. That doesn't mean the fish that are feeding on the bugs being swept off them are always sitting in the riffle itself (that's why we track the foam lanes below the riffle/food source). Also, there will be times when terrestrial bugs fall on the water from particular species of plants or trees. Looking at wind directions that deliver those bugs to the water - and then the subsequent foam lane carrying them downstream - lets you link up the food source to the "food delivery" route.

In the second question, we are really asking how a **spot where a fish is likely to lie** maps onto those food lanes. I am very fond of saying that the most interesting stuff in biology happens at the edges. It's always the boundaries between contrasting situations/states/structures that concentrates biological activity.

As a quick-start guide, pick anything you like from the following examples of boundaries:

- Light/Shade
- Deep/Shallow
- Fast/Slow
- Foam/Open water
- Rock/Water

Any and all of those boundaries can be hotspots for fish on any given day. When a potential hotspot has a food conveyor-belt running past it, then that is prime fishy real-estate.

As a final note on building up your stream-reading skills, there is often a pattern of fish preferring deeper/slower water when that water is cold. The reverse is also true, with faster/shallower water being a good bet in warm weather. It's not guaranteed, but it is worth STARTING in the depth of water suggested by the temperature, before experimenting. Of course, if you can see fish rising, then that takes care of reading the water right away.

Single Dry Fly

This fly fishing staple probably needs no introduction. While we can all **continually improve our fish-spotting abilities**; once we have seen a fish rise then it is our fly casting and drift-control skills that are likely to determine success or failure. Particularly that idea of "not screwing up before the fish sees our fly" by:

- Not allowing our casting line to drift over the fish before it has seen our fly (positioning sense - where to cast from)

- Not ripping the line off the water to re-cast (draw it slowly off to one side of the feeding lane and pick of delicately when you've retrieved enough line)

- Not dumping the line down heavily onto the water helps to avoid spooking our target fish - and others we've not seen- (use less power than you think, aim a foot or more above the surface of the stream)

Also, don't make the mistake of only ever casting at the same angle to the current. Where rules allow, dry fly fishing should be a 360-degree activity. Sending the fly downstream ahead of your tippet and casting line lets the fish see your fly before anything else. Your casting angle and position should be determined by how you need to control your line after the fly has landed - not by a text-book/pre-prescribed recipe.

My other tips are to be confident fishing (particularly slightly bushier flies) on the surface - even when fish are not rising. Small streams tend to be shallower than larger rivers - and a quick trip to the surface from the river bed isn't as much effort when the distance is so short. When fishing "blind" like this, target features in the same way as you would with a sunk fly (revisit those reading the water tips as necessary). Also, be happy to modify flies on-stream. I've had great sport in fading light with trout sipping Blue Wing Olive spinners by clipping the hackle above and below the shank on a little Ishigaki and greasing it up to float. Finally, if tiny flies aren't working, try going to the totally opposite end of the scale with a BIG, "shocker" dry fly.

Duo/Hopper-Dropper

Beware if you think this is "chuck it and chance it" fishing. For instance, doing it well means that you never really suspend the nymph below the dry fly. Instead the nymph should sink down and, by the time you are picking off the water, only just be reaching towards the position of hanging directly below the dry fly.

As suggested in my suggested fly selection, using that Retirer variant is a great option for the buoyant dry fly on the dropper. If visibility isn't good enough with the standard dressing, feel free to alter the elk hair or deer hair wing colour to something easier to see. Here's a suggested rig with tippet-measurements:

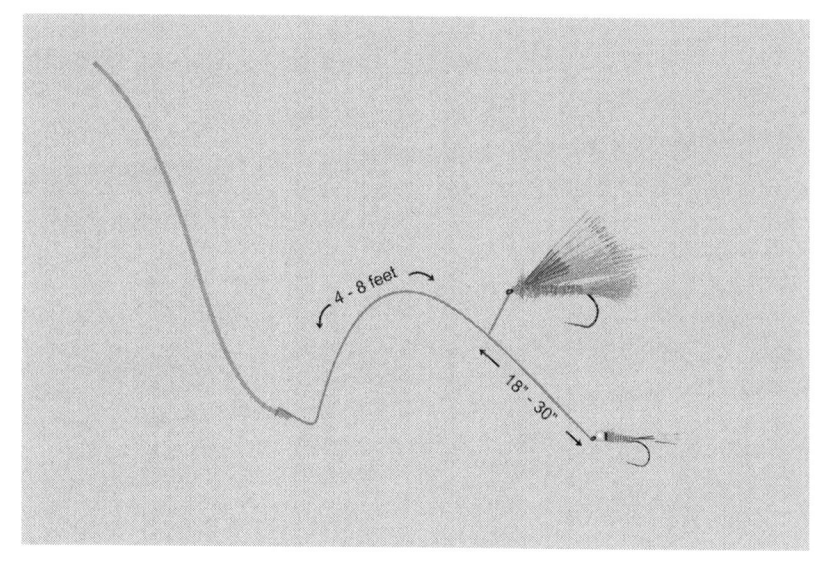

While there are a surprising number of layers to this technique, knowing a handful of things will really improve your success. One of the most important things is to keep drifts as short as possible (aiming for 3 to 5 seconds where you can). Your nymph will need to reach the desired fishing depth during that time - which is another good reason for having several bead-weights and profiles of nymph. A second game-changer for this tactic is to always, where possible, hold all the fly line and all the tippet off the water - right up to the dry fly whenever you can. That gives brilliant drifts (reaching over any complex currents) and it creates a much better contact for good hook-sets when a fish grabs one of your flies. It also reduces the chances of spooking fish with your line (either floating overhead or - worse- being ripped off the water when setting the hook).

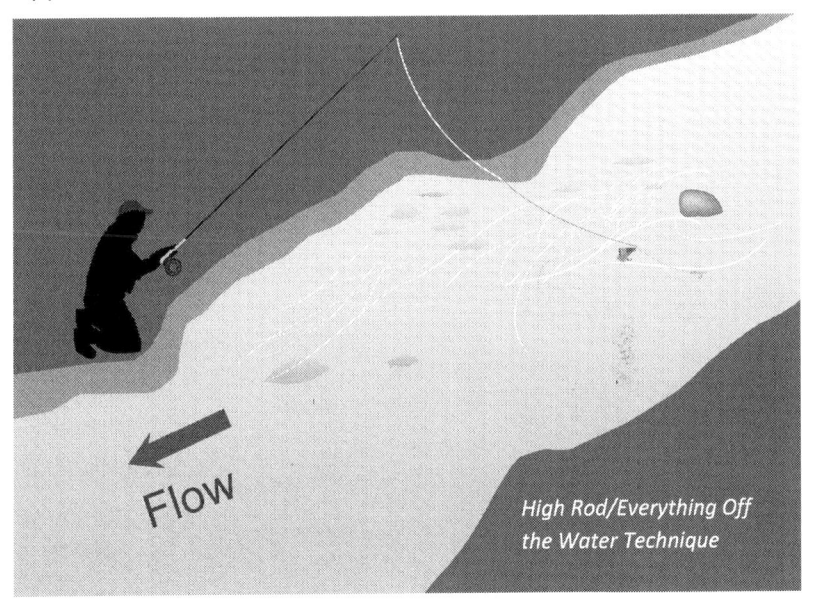

High Rod/Everything Off the Water Technique

Double and Single Nymph or Wet Fly

Can be fished by knotting tippet onto a standard fly line - or also by using one of the specialist casting lines covered in #6 out of this book's Top 10 Tips (Tip #6, p35). For ultimate stealth, you will stick to a single fly. I've already described the trick of using a sight spider for really spooky fish (or just for fun). Whether that fly is an unweighted wet fly, bead-head or shrimp/scud is obviously down to the feeding depth/mood of the fish on the day.

Double flies can allow funky combinations of weighted tail fly (point fly) and unweighted/tiny dropper fly when necessary. For casting upstream, I would always put the heaviest fly on the point to prevent the situation where my point fly overtakes my dropper during the drift. Fishing downstream under some tension (as shown in the downstream presentations from our **Fly Manipulations** content), then you can choose whether the heaviest fly goes on the point or dropper position. If you can't see the fish eat the fly, just watch for any twitch or hesitation of the tip of your casting line - that's your cue to set the hook.

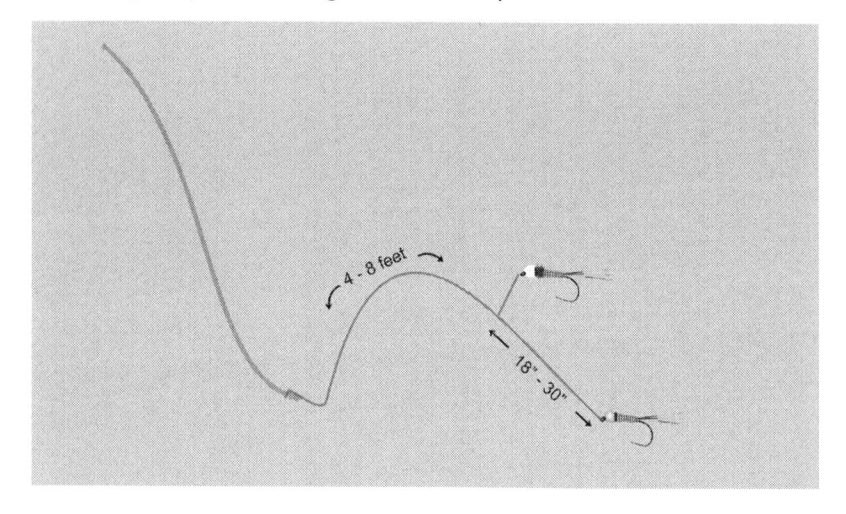

Double or single nymphing/wet-fly is generally better when most of the feeding activity is sub-surface. Duo/Hopper-Dropper is great for a couple of other situations. Firstly, the obvious one where both the dry and the nymph are equally likely to be eaten by the fish.

The second situation is when you need to reach straight across the current and have the dry fly "pilot" your nymph downstream into (or past) a specific feature. You tend to get a much more "in-line with the current" drift with the Duo/Hopper-Dropper rig for that (especially when using a high rod-tip position).

Streamer Fishing

I suppose the first thing to say is to not neglect streamers on little rivers. Trout and other game fish are very capable of eating baitfish that are a third - or even close to half - their own body length. A single streamer fished through the best (and deepest) holes on a small stream can throw up some real surprise specimen fish. At the same time, it is a great way of catching just the regular-sized fish in a little stream too.

I tend to fish streamers on a single-fly rig for small streams (there are some other things I might mix and match with on larger rivers). You can readily fish a streamer on just the same setup that you'd use for single dry fly (i.e. the most standard fly fishing rig in the world). I would increase the tippet strength a bit - just to help you get your fly back when it snags. With an increase in the size and weight of the fly, your tippet tends to fade into the background when a trout's attention is caught by the "prey image" of a streamer. That distraction means there is little or no downside to using stronger tippet.

It is also really effective to fish a streamer on a French Leader (or another of the specialist lines mentioned in Tip #6). In fact that setup opens up a lot of those Top 10 tips to give you a significant edge on-stream.

Streamer with:
French Leader (top)
Regular Fly Line (bottom)

Tactics: Key Components

While it is impossible to do justice to all the deep detail of each individual technique given here, just being aware of these go-to options is a big advantage. When it comes to things like fly choice, method choice and biological-trigger-based techniques (like using the *super-normal stimuli* (!!?) effect of bright orange and pink shrimp patterns); the book "**How to Fool Fish with Simple Flies**" lays out a detailed system.

However, there are some basic components that will set you up for success with the tactics and flies featured in this book...

For very (VERY) broad guidance, I would tend to use tippets in the 5x and 6x range for most dry fly fishing. On rare occasions, I might have to go to 7x for midge fishing. For the nymphing, wet-flies and duo/hopper-dropper a common diameter would be around 5x.

That being said, larger wet flies and small streamers are a good match for 4x tippet.

When it comes to leader and tippet length - the shorter the connection between fly and end of casting line; the more strike indication you have. That usually needs to be balanced against the chances of spooking fish with fly-line splashdown. Using a longer leader creates more separation between fly line disturbance and your fly. It can also make it more likely that your fly will end up in a tree. A good compromise for dry flies, small streamers and single wet flies fished on a fly line can be the use of light, short furled leaders and low (sub AFTM #2) fly lines. Alternatively, the high rod tip/everything off the water approach used with French Leaders and Duo/Hopper-Dropper rigs simply takes line-splash out of the equation entirely.

Finally, just taking the most basic precautions to avoid casting your shadow on the water, avoiding heavy footfalls (or just walking well away from the area you're about to fish) will reward you with so many fish that other anglers miss out on. Keeping all this in mind, it's time to hit you with the Top 10 Tips...

Top 10 Tips...Starting with #1. Use the LONGEST Rod Possible

Look, I know it is often said that you need little rods for these little streams. I might also admit that the "longest" rod possible in some conditions could be six feet (or even less). However, you hear all the time - *"ooh, you'll need a six-foot-six rod for that stream"* - on waters where we'll normally fish a 10' 6" rod.

I get it. Casting and playing fish under tree-cover often has less chance of the tip clashing with branches when you're fishing a shorter rod. However, you are giving away a massive amount of line control with every foot of rod that you lose. That means you're probably less likely to have the problem of avoiding branches while playing fish (more on this very soon) - but only because you'll not be hooking fish in the first place.

With a long rod, it is easier to perform the essential tight-quarters casting tactics that we'll be covering in a few pages and - most of all - a longer rod allows you to reach and hold line off the water. For reasons of both stealth (ESSENTIAL in close-quarters fishing) and drift control, holding casting line and even tippet off the water are massive advantages.

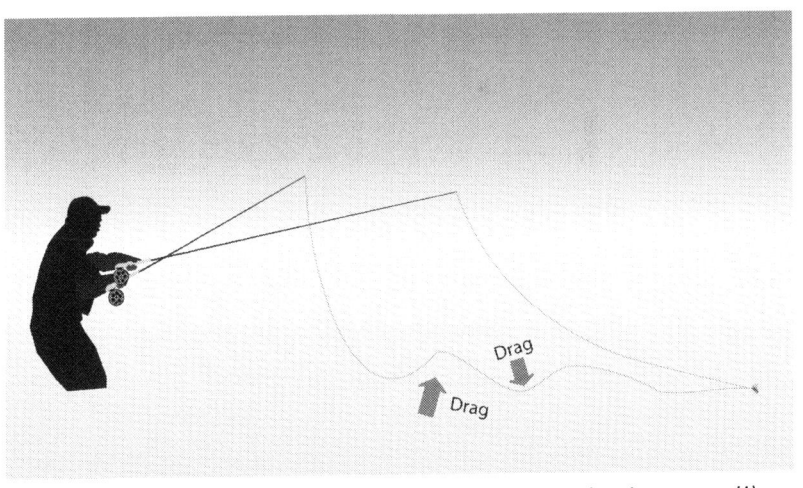

Hold your line off the water (much more effective with a longer rod!)

Holding line off the water not only avoids line splash (that can scare fish) and avoids tricky, nagging currents that spoil your drift - it also creates a much more direct "contact" when setting the hook. You don't need to overcome the surface tension of the water on the line - so it is much more efficient and effective.

Something that many anglers don't realise is how helpful a longer rod can be when fishing under low, overhanging branches on the opposite bank. Being able to "reach" in underneath that canopy can create a great advantage by allowing you to shorten the amount of line between the rod-tip and the fly.

Again that short line/long rod situation gives you the contact, stealth and good drift that always comes with the ability to keep casting line off the water. You just need to remember to use a sideways movement to set the hook when a fish grabs hold.

You'll also need to use side-strain to "kite" the fish out from underneath the overhanging branches.

Then it's a case of either backing up to find a spot where you can raise the rod up to bring the fish to the net - or else use the sneaky tactic described next...

2. Use "Hand-lining" Under Low Canopy

This "get out of jail" tactic is brilliant for landing fish under low canopy. It is also great to have it well-practiced for any time you might get your line jammed and are unable to retrieve line through the guides to stay in contact with a fish.

Although a little difficult to explain in words, the combined description and images should make it possible to include this technique in your own fishing. Do bear in mind though - even if you are shown how to do this in person - you still need to practice it several times in easy conditions before it is workable in tight-quarters fishing.

Perhaps the most important element is that, if you know you can't get your rod vertical to land a fish, you should try to go to this technique as soon as possible after hooking up. This is due to the fact that, if the fish runs to the far bank (and you can't easily wade towards that opposite bank) then it may be almost impossible to grab the line.

The first step, then is to sweep the rod tip low to the water and out behind you so that it draws the line close to your shins.

Aim to put your body directly between the fish and your (low) rod-tip

You can then reach outwards (and downwards) with your non-rod hand - palm facing out towards the fish. Sweeping your arm and hand in a small circular motion against the taught line lets you slide that line along the outer edge of your forearm or hand until you can close your fingers OVER THE TOP of the line

Use the outside "blade" of your hand/forearm to make contact with the line before taking a light grip on it by circling your fingers round on top of it.

Once you have a LIGHT GRIP on the line - bring your rod-hand (along with the rod butt) down to meet your non-rod hand. This lets you take a grip with the **index finger of your rod hand** as well as holding the line in the **palm of your non-rod hand**.

The most difficult part is quickly and reliably making the initial line-catch using the circular motion of your non-rod-hand. The second pitfall is avoiding the instinct to clamp down with a "death grip" onto the line once you've caught it. If the fish is a strong one, you may well need to give line through your fingers as you are trying to pull the fish towards you. That is why we emphasise a soft, light grip on the line.

You can see how both hands work together to gather the line in the following pictures.

Gripping the line with a "trigger" grip in the crook of your index finger is a great way to control the pressure on the line

You can either draw the line through that trigger finger grip with your non-rod hand - or else you can pass the line from hand to hand as you gather it in. The first option is safer and more reliable, the second allows a faster maximum speed of line retrieval.

As mentioned, everything from catching the line through to smoothly gathering it is something that needs practice in ideal conditions before it becomes familiar enough to do on autopilot. You'll find that there are a LOT of distractions when you have a thrashing fish and the obstacles of a small stream to cope with. That is not the time to start "learning on the job"!

3. Catapult or Slingshot Cast

Yes this is a classic standby and pretty much essential for any small stream addict. Just remember to open out the angle of the rod blank towards you before pulling back on the line. You don't want to pull the rod tip directly back on itself. That is a recipe for a broken rod.

To do this, cock your rod-hand wrist backwards as you draw back the tippet/line/fly with your non rod-hand. Then, as you release the fly, straighten your wrist and point your thumb at your target.

This creates accuracy and control of the line. As well as avoiding the need for any space for a back-cast, this tactic also massively reduces the amount of swinging back and forth you need to do with the rod. All told, it makes it much less likely that you'll bash your rod or tangle your line with the vegetation.

4. Roll Cast

Another absolute essential for tight-quarters fishing. Again, requiring very little back-cast space and minimising how much you need to wave the rod around.

With practice you can modify this cast a great deal - so that you can choose how to position and move the "D-loop" at many different angles behind the rod. This allows you to put that loop of line into the available gaps in the vegetation and load the rod.

It is also a great cast for changing the direction of the forward cast - so it helps you deliver a fly at different points over the cross-section of the stream.

Practicing this on grass between fishing sessions is really worthwhile - because the ability to do a good roll-cast with only the fly anchored on the surface when you form a D-loop is a big advantage. The most common faults include trying to push the rod tip too far forward on the delivery (instead aim the forward cast above the surface of the water with a high "stop").

The second thing that holds people back - especially when practicing on grass or only anchoring the fly on the water - is the need for a "slip" on the forward cast. This is where you slide your rod-hand forward while keeping your wrist cocked back in the "telephone answer" position. Then, right at the point where you want to "tap" the cast high and forward, you point your wrist straight to create that "snap" and deliver the cast.

5. Side-cast under canopy

Sometimes useful when you need more line-speed (perhaps punching into a head-wind) or when it is really difficult to create a roll-cast because of super-low overhanging branches all around.

In its most basic form, this is simply a standard overhead cast that you have rotated so that the rod is moving parallel to the water. That, alone, is certainly good enough to give you an advantage - though there is a really great tweak to increase your catch rate by a huge factor.

First cast the line parallel to the water as normal. You can even make it travel under the rod tip if you like - **as in the photo above** (check out the FFM Italian Style of Casting for that). Then, just as you deliver the forward cast, bring the rod tip up as high as you can so that only the fly lands on the water. Basically, you are aiming to finish in the perfect "line and leader off the water" fishing position.

First begin your side-cast as normal - by casting parallel to the water it is possible to "measure" your cast and get a good feel for whether your fly will land on target (an advantage over the roll cast where you only get one chance). Note, this loop is also "upside down" - travelling below the rod tip AND the "bottom-leg" of the casting loop is highest off the water.

Then, right at the point that you're delivering the final forward cast, bring your rod up smoothly to the finishing "fishing position" with a high rod-tip (at least as high as the canopy will allow). This prevents any splash-down

A 10-foot 6-inch AFTM #3 rod & single wet-fly pattern fished in tight canopy

6. Choose a Specialist Casting Line or Leader

Many people don't realise that, as long as the rod is not too stiff, you can use the European competition anglers' "French Leaders" on shorter fly rods too (amazing for holding line off the water). So, let's say that an 8-foot rod is the longest that is possible for you in a particular stream - you can definitely throw a French leader with confidence on rods rated for AFTM #3 and below.

That is a great small-stream rig for small dry flies, wet flies, nymphs and - surprisingly - a single streamer too. In fact, carrying some small to medium size streamers should probably be a small-stream commandment in its self! They can be tremendous at pulling the "daddy" of the pool and a great tactic when nothing is hatching.

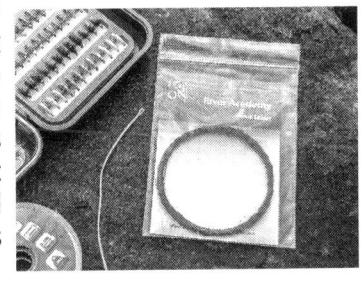

A trick that so many **fly rod and reel** anglers miss out on is to avoid the specialist casting lines designed for Japanese tenkara. It is easy to **attach these to the end of your fly line** and use them like a French Leader. Whether it is the fluorocarbon level line (I advise a #3.5 on the Japanese diameter scale) or even a specially-manufactured tapered nylon line; these are awesome weapons when paired with a light-line fly rod. They can allow you to cast larger, more wind-resistant dry flies as well as coping better in a wind than a regular French leader.

For the factory-tapered nylon lines our recommendation would be for the "Fujino" tenkara lines anywhere in 4.5 to 7-m range of lengths. Our favourites are the green "midi" lines and the ice-blue special lines which have a longer, delicate front taper.

You can cast all of these lines on a rod & reel setup **using all the casting tactics we talk about in this book**. Professional casting coaching can also really help your success.

7. Use Currents to Fish "Impossible" Spots

There are certain places on small streams that are a total graveyard for flies. I'm sure you can think of plenty. These are lies where your fly needs to fish tight up against the bank but the hot-spot is surrounded by tangled vegetation as well as a protective "roof" of overhanging branches.

When you get really good at catapult casting, you can measure off exactly the length of line that you need and get really good at threading casts into tight spots. However, in some spots, even that approach is a low percentage game.

For those places, it is time to call on one of my favourite sneaky dodges. It needs you to have a really good sense of positioning - in other words getting a good feel of exactly where to stand to give you an unfair advantage. The idea is that, by being a "current detective" you can find helpful patches of flow that will carry your fly *towards* the target.

Often this means getting out of the stream, working round into position and then dropping a cast into the flow A SAFE DISTANCE UPSTREAM of the obstacle. Then you need to feed enough slack into the line to let the stream carry your fly underneath and between the snags - deep into the "impossible" lair.

It goes without saying that these spots often hold the biggest fish of those streams - since they are great habitat for avoiding natural predators (as well as avoiding anglers' flies).

Personally I find this tactic one of the most nerve-wracking things you can do on stream. As you send your fly to "hitch a lift" on the conveyer-belt that carries it into the danger zone...every nerve is stretched taut. If the little bobbing artificial is carried past all the hazards and snags and manages to continue on into the sweet spot; then the weight of anticipation

"Small stream" does not necessarily mean small fish

is absolutely crushing. It's almost an unbearable pressure to see that fly disappear in a large swirl - knowing you need to set the hook sideways with a low rod-tip if you are to stand any chance of avoiding the branches...Not for the faint of heart.

8. Fish Downstream More Often than you Might Think

This one might seem weird once you have got to the point where you realise how deadly it can be to fish wet flies, nymphs and dries on a dead drift. Typically this involves casting up (or perhaps up and across) the stream. Tracking the fly/flies either back towards you or across your position with a high rod-tip is often a recipe for fantastic sport.

Ok, there are plenty of folks who never do anything other than swing wet flies down and across the current with a low rod tip. Sure, you'll get pulls and nips and enough fish to keep you interested by doing that - but that is absolutely not what I am talking about here. Instead, I mean this in a more thoughtful way. The previous example ("commandment" #7), often relies on fishing downstream.

What I am really talking about is concentrating on being stealthy, being prepared to fish a "downstream dead drift", often using a high rod-tip position and really THINKING your fly downstream through various features. If you're using a sub-surface pattern - try hard to see that fly in your mind's eye as it travels down through likely spots. Make sure to take full advantage of your ability to choose the pace that your fly travels. That could be a full dead drift or some modified pace of your choice. It is much more difficult to have much control over drift pace when casting upstream - and it can be a huge advantage.

Another advantage is that the fish is likely to see your fly before

it sees either your line or your rod-tip. The downsides (as there must always be - there is no one single perfect technique) include a greater difficulty in hooking fish and also a need to take more care to stay hidden from the fish.

9. In Tight Streams - Pick a Direction and Work it

Your chosen stream might have high, inaccessible banks (maybe even high walls in the case of urban streams) or dense ranks of trees on both sides. In these cases, it is often either impossible or really counterproductive to keep getting in and out of the stream. Even where it is possible, the chances of disturbing fish before you ever get to show them a fly are just too high. Instead, you should use your best guess to pick the most favourable overall direction to fish (i.e. upstream or downstream presentations). Obviously, this might depend on how much prior knowledge you have of the stream you're tackling.

If you know a stream well, it makes your decision pretty easy (unless you want to deliberately challenge yourself in an effort to up your game). For unfamiliar waters you might have enough map or satellite image data to clue you in on several access points. In those cases, you could choose to work upstream for one section - before walking ahead (out of the stream) and then working back downstream along the next section.

Where you know almost nothing about the stream you're about to fish, I would tend to prefer to start at the upstream limit and work downstream. This is simply because, on a tight/tricky stream, you'll find a lot of advantages in being able to choose the pace of presentation.

An exception to that general guideline would be on a steep, boulder-canyon where the only way up is really to climb the stream. Another exception might be a really slow-flowing watercourse where you'd kick up a lot of sediment. In that situation (if you can't fish from the bank) then you have little choice but to fish upstream.

Overall, the best thing you can do is develop well-rounded skills in fishing in all directions to the current. That lets you be completely comfortable when you're forced to stay in the channel and work one specific direction for a prolonged period.

Of course, the more knowledge and tactics that you can discover and carry with you - then the better your results and experience will be. While that sounds fairly obvious - so few of us really do this because it is human nature to find anything new/outside our familiar limits as fairly horrifying. How to combat this?

Wild fish from small streams can have unbelievable markings

10. Two Anglers to a Rod

In answer to the question about "how to make the unfamiliar attractive" - picking a good fishing buddy can be a fantastic advantage. The key detail, though, is that you should only fish with one rod between the two of you. There are multiple advantages to this:

- Better Stealth in Small Streams (you don't scare anywhere near as many fish before getting a fly to them)

- Observing someone else fish - it is difficult to see our own strengths and faults from inside our own skin, but much easier to assess effective techniques when watching from the outside

- The opportunity to get feedback from that third person perspective (having comments is really helpful)

- Allowing observation of the stream when you are normally preoccupied with actually fishing

- Teamwork, banter and good fun in the shared experience

Overall, this friendly "workshopping" is both fun and also really effective. It makes it much easier to try out and assess new/strange tactics and it really does make it easier to spot fish and also **minimise your chances of spooking fish**.

Perhaps the biggest recommendation is the enjoyment factor - sharing the inevitable ups and downs of fishing for wild trout in tricky settings is a wonderful thing. Whether it is a friendly competitive edge or a totally "team effort" approach, then these kind of trips always have the potential to create brilliant fishing stories and memories.

Sharing a rod can also help you stick to, and take advantage of, many of the other tips included in this guide.

If you're hungry for more (and to go a little deeper) - you're in luck...

Researching & Finding New Small Streams to Fish

In the age of big-data and ever-expanding online information sources, there are a lot of tools that are really helpful to the small stream angler. At the time of writing, there are some amazing tools that are completely free to use. However, with great power comes great responsibility! So here are some ground rules:

Rules of Engagement:

- **No Trespassing**
- **No Poaching (fishing without permission)**
- **No Over-exploitation (C&R with Barbless Hooks Only - and also leave un-fished gaps when having a good day)**
- **No breaking local rules, laws or regulations**

I'm not about to have anyone use this book as an excuse to compromise access, sporting or land-ownership rights. In other words, please take this as a formal notice that it's *your* responsibility to make sure you are entitled to access and fish any streams that you discover. *Laws vary between countries*.

Now, if we're all agreed on the above? OK, let's dive in to some tools that can help you. Be aware that these are not the only options - and that you'll continue to discover new or different resources all the time. Overall, the important thing is the approach you take to understanding information provided by these amazing datasets.

Suggested Tools

I'll first of all list out four main tools as well as two subsidiary tools before explaining each one in turn. As mentioned above, if these tools become unavailable or are replaced by others;

often the overall approach will still allow you to get what you need. Here's the list of six to get you off to the races:

Main Tools

- Google Maps' "Special Features"
- Google Earth/Satellite
- BGS Geology Map Viewer
- USGS Geologic Map/Mineral Resources Interactive Maps

Subsidiary Tools

- OpenSignal.com
- Magic GIS (UK Only)

If you already know one (or more) of the tools in the above list inside and out, you can obviously skip that section in the following guidance.

Google Maps' "Special Features"
https://www.google.com/maps

I don't want to give the impression that regular maps are yesterday's news. Far from it - one of the best things you can do when you've homed in on an area that seems promising is to buy a large-scale printed map.

So whether you're using the standard online maps (including Google's products) or a printed map - there is a basic check list of information that you're after that includes:

- Distance from nearest road
- Accessible by in-stream-wading/climbing only or by path?
- Sinuosity
- Longitudinal Bed-slope (estimate)

- Elevation

- Upstream Conditions (dam-releases, water quality associated with land-use)

- Nearby properties

- Ground Cover/Vegetation

- Nearest Camping/shelter

The thing that I want to make sure you're aware of is a feature within Google Maps that may not be immediately obvious. That is the inclusion of elevation data via contour lines - which is not usually a visible layer when you browse their maps (at the time of writing at least).

To access it you need to go to Google Maps (link under the sub-heading for this section) and click the "Menu" icon at the top left (right now this icon is three horizontal lines).

The drop-down menu that appears contains an option called "Terrain". When you click on that, it enables a small toggle switch at the bottom of the Google Map that you go on to browse. That switch is labelled "Terrain, View Topography and Elevation" and clicking it to slide it to the right reveals a layer of shading and contour lines.

Now, it looks like Google's terms and conditions require me to request and pay for extra special permission to include a series of screenshots inside a product for sale (like this book). So what I've done is simply sketched a map out in some drawing software (next page) to walk through **assessing how steep a river is**. My sketch doesn't have the lovely shaded 3-D effects of the maps you'll see on Google, but I hope it does the job of illustrating a point.

Obviously, the concept is something that will be familiar to anyone who is used to reading maps - but what might trip you up is where labelling of values differs from your usual maps.

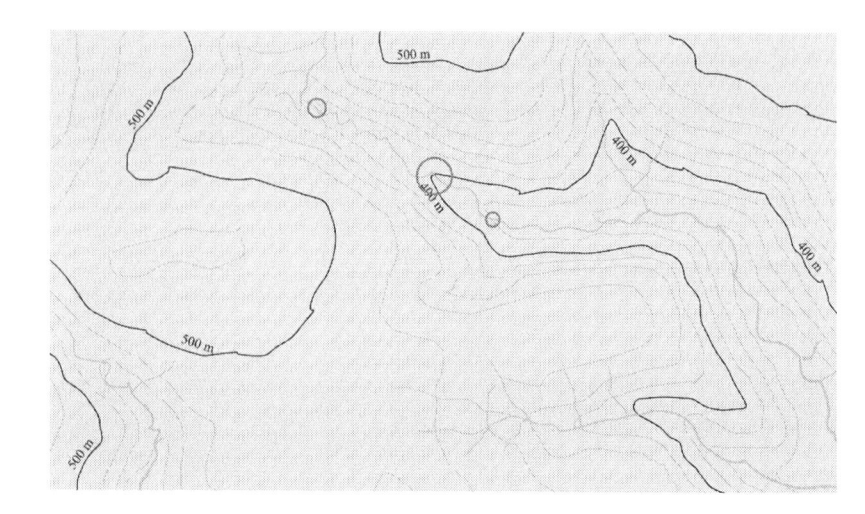

It is really useful to get a feel for the longitudinal bed-slope of a stream before you fish it. Not only will it predict how tough your hike is likely to be, it also gives you clues on the type of features and water you'll be fishing. As an added bonus, you can also see exactly what elevation(s) you'll be at - so you can gauge that against likely temperature under the weather conditions on the day.

The sketch map above has three small circles on it. Each circle marks the point at which a river crosses a contour line. Of those three - the largest, central, circle relates to the darker and thicker 400-m contour line.

Maps on Google at this scale have contour lines that are 20-m apart. When you zoom out further, they jump to 40-m apart. The comparable local printed maps will usually have contours that are 5 or 10-m apart. It's just something to watch out for and is easy to spot by just counting the number of paler contour lines between each major/dark line. Since you can jump five gaps from the 500-m contour to the 400-m contour - it makes each gap equal to a 20-m change in elevation.

By combining the scale that is provided on each map page with that elevation data, it is fairly easy to calculate bed-slope. It is just a case of dividing the vertical distance (the rise) by the horizontal distance (the run).

If you multiply that ratio by 100, then you can express that slope as a percentage.

That way, you can choose to look at the overall average slope between two widely-spaced points (e.g. the distance between the two small circles on the sketch map). Alternatively, you can home in on the slope of individual reaches within that longer section of stream. Examples of that would be calculating the slope between the left-hand small circle and the large, central circle (and doing a separate calculation for the central circle to the right-hand circle).

What does slope tell you anyway?
With shallower slopes, you can expect a river to meander more and to have more diversity in the cross-sectional profile of the riverbed. The formation of scour pools on the outside of bends below riffles can result in some bigger fish. If the map shows a channel straighter than you'd expect, then that stream is likely to have been modified by engineers. It may have poorer fishing as a result.

With naturally-steep channels, expect strong flows, plunge pools and exciting boulder-strewn runs with complex currents. The steeper a channel is, the less it will naturally meander. Put simply, gravity is able to pull it straight down with less influence of friction to steer that water left and right. The fast pace of water in a steep stream will strongly erode and mobilise stream-bed material - with larger boulders and banks creating friction that encourages localised deposits of gravels. As long as the elevation is sufficient to maintain year-round cool water (and in the absence of pollution/other impacts), then these types of stream will tend to hold lots of trout and char.

Having noted the basic shape, slope and features marked on the map, it's time to switch views to get more specific...

Google Satellite View
Accessible within Google Maps

From the Google Maps Menu (where we found the "Terrain" option), click on "Satellite" to see aerial photography of the area of interest.

This lets us build out some details directly from images of the stream itself. There is, of course, a limit to the resolution and clarity of these images. The one I've mocked up on this page should give a sense of that resolution - albeit in black and white

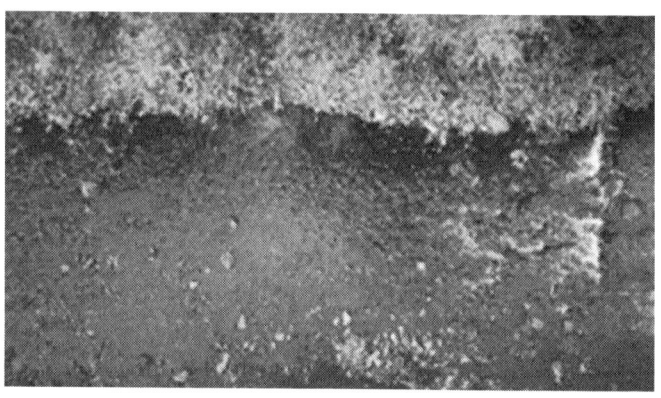

rather than colour. As was the case with the map data, I'd need special permission to reproduce Google's own satellite images here.

Here are some of the things you can lay onto your existing detective work:

Tree Canopy Cover - both on surrounding land and over the channel. You should be able to tell whether that tree cover is mostly coniferous or deciduous. In turn that can tell you what kind of invertebrate detritus-feeders will be supported in your stream. In the UK, deciduous forests tend to produce a range of leaf litter that is more palatable/digestible by aquatic fungi and bugs. They also tend to produce more terrestrial bugs that fall into the water to subsidise the diet of trout and other fish. In other parts of the world, where coniferous species occur in diverse (i.e. not planted in dense monoculture) stands, these can create nutritious inputs for aquatic foodwebs too. Some research and local knowledge into those factors will help to make sense of forests shown on satellite images.

In-stream Features: Pools, riffles, glides, boulder cascades - even changes in depth over the channel cross-section can all be seen on the satellite view. Those food conveyor belts - and potential "edges" that I introduced in the reading the water section - may also be visible. As well as the existence of those features, you can get a sense of how frequent they are and how spread out or close together they occur. That sense of feature-density should translate well into fish-number predictions. Highly featured streams tend to hold more game fish than uniform channels lacking structure and varied current-speeds/depths.

Water Colour: Whether whiskey-stained (probably acidic) or clear/blue (more neutral or alkaline), the colour of the water is very useful to know. Whatever the colour, deeper water tends to be possible to identify by being darker. Clear streams may allow you to see how much weed is present and the way it is distributed.

Surrounding land-use/Possible Pollution: Depending on how recently the image was taken, the current status could differ from what is shown on Google Maps. That being said, the presence of some long-term pressures are likely to be visible. Whether the stream has a vegetated buffer strip to separate it from intensive grazing or forestry is one example. Another may be obvious sediment/nutrient pollution inputs created by livestock drinking points.

Underlying Geology (BGS and USGS)
http://mapapps.bgs.ac.uk/geologyofbritain/home.html *BGS*
https://mrdata.usgs.gov/geology/state/ *USGS*

One of the real "secret weapons" for a small stream detective is the existence of detailed interactive maps of the surface and underlying geology of river basins. Not only will that give clues to the water chemistry and associated productivity - it will also indicate how rich and diverse the surrounding terrestrial vegetation should be too.

The way these mapping tools work is basically the same - you can pan and zoom around the maps and then click on the various coloured layers to bring up the associated data. Depending on the site, you might also be able to turn the map key on and off. Turning it on allows you to match the colour you see with particular types of rock. Turning it off can free up more space for you to see the whole map more easily.

Here is a sample of what is likely to come up when you click on a shaded area on a map (with notes in bold):

Smithville Dolomite, Powell Dolomite, Cotter Dolomite, Jefferson City Dolomite (**These are the rock types included in that shaded area**)

Fine crystalline, silty, cherty dolomite, and oolitic chert with local sandstone beds. (**Here is a general characterisation**)

State: Missouri (**Location**)

Geologic age: Early Ordovician-Ibexian Series (**Age of rock**)

Lithologic constituents (**Breakdown of rock types**)

Major

Sedimentary > Carbonate > Dolostone (Bed)

Minor

Sedimentary > Clastic > Mudstone > Shale (Bed)

Sedimentary > Clastic > Sandstone (Bed)

Sedimentary > Chemical > Chert (Bed)

So what does all this mean? Probably the simplest and most useful things to understand are the rock types that are associated with higher productivity (limestone and chalk) versus harsher, more-acidic conditions (gritstone, coal measures, granite, rhyolite). If in doubt, a quick internet search for "What kind of soil does X produce" - where "X" is the highest level description of the rock type - should help.

Calcareous rivers are more productive - and you can expect bigger fish in any streams with base-rich/alkaline water chemistry. However, alkaline water amplifies the toxicity of ammonia that is found, for example, in sewage effluent. This can be a major consideration when researching small urban chalkstreams versus urban upland/peat-stained streams.

Streams with slightly acidic waters can still produce great numbers of fish - and certainly specimen fish are a reasonable expectation. However, the average size tends to be a bit smaller than chalk and limestone streams. They often make up in numbers for what they might lack in average size though.

I know that experts could read a lot more into the complex interaction between geology and ecological community data than I've explained here. On the other hand, I hope you'll agree that it is possible for anyone to find out tons of useful information before they ever cast a line on a particular stream... So, Rounding off this theme, here are two final tools that you might find useful to your specific situation.

Open Signal
https://www.opensignal.com/networks

Travelling into unknown areas, an important safety consideration is whether you'll have any cellphone coverage - or not. The searchable and extensively zoomable maps shown on Opensignal.com were also extremely useful for us when we needed to research network coverage for a live TV broadcast in Japan! It's certainly worth getting a feel for what kind of emergency signal you might (or might NOT) have on your expedition.

Magic (GIS) - UK only
https://magic.defra.gov.uk/MagicMap.aspx

There are an impressive number of data-layers on this UK-based interactive map. As well as high-level conservation/scientific designations, there's also stuff like priority habitats and species, Countryside Stewardship areas and historic designations too.

Of course, those things all help with predictions of water quality and the kinds of habitats and characteristics you'd expect to find. However, those datasets can also be really valuable in bottoming out the permissions and access side of things.

The other thing that Magic does fantastically well is their screen-measurement tool. It allows you to draw either paths or enclosed areas with multiple points at any scale on the map. Perhaps you want to get a good estimate of how wide a small stream is? Or maybe you want details on how long a twisting path (or river) actually is? Once you've clicked away at your required points (and the little line of flag icons is complete), then it instantly kicks out the figure you specify. In my experience, the results are pretty darn accurate too.

Coupling those measurements with terrain/slope information might just help you to make good decisions about how tough and how long a trip is likely to be.

OK, that is enough to be going on with. I know that there are more fantastic tools - particularly since some members of the "Small Streams" multimedia bundle website have shared some of their favourites! However what I've outlined here should give you plenty to get your teeth into. It is also a good chance for me to highlight the Small Streams Mastery membership/multimedia site - and two associated publications...

Onstream Video & E-books of Small Stream Maestro #1: Kazunori Kobayashi

Along with your free Youtube episodes and email tutorials, Kobayashi-san's **premium videos** and **e-books** cover his small stream approach - from flies to tackle and tactics on this link:

https://doublebadgers.kartra.com/page/smallstreams35

The small-stream angler is completely spoiled for choice in Japan. BUT - the fishing can be super difficult because of the shy fish and clear water. Most streams see high numbers of anglers taking fish for the table. The low density of fish that remain are, as a result, the most difficult to catch.

It is on those unforgiving streams that Kazunori Kobayashi honed his impressive small-stream skills. *Find out what we discovered when he opened up his box of tricks and tactics to us in 2017...*

Re-discover "Lost" Tactics of Small Stream Maestro #2: Henry Charles Cutcliffe

As part of the multi-media bundle on the previous page, you will also discover the tactics of an overlooked master small stream angler of the 1800's.

Cutcliffe's book was cited by non other than **G.E.M. Skues himself** as one of only five works he considered *"...really indispensible for a dresser of trout and grayling flies to have"*, this expert angler of North Devon's small streams is virtually unknown in the world of fly fishing today.

I've spent **a year unravelling the tactics, flies and rigs of this frighteningly effective stream fisher** and created an illustrated decoding of his original 1863 manuscript that is easy to understand and apply by the modern angler. A condensed e-book version of Cutcliffe's manuscript formed part of the "early bird" bonus content in the "Small Streams Mastery" Bundle:

https://doublebadgers.kartra.com/page/smallstreams35

The Print version of *"Fly Fishing Master H.C. Cutcliffe Rediscovered in The Art of Trout Fishing in Rapid Streams"* includes a **full photographic record of his flies** is available to buy on Amazon today.

Small Streams Fishing Trip Log

Date:	Grid ref:	☀ ☁ ⛈

Hatch Notes

Water Temp:	Flow: L M H	Water Color: Clear Stained Muddy

Fish Caught

Trip Notes

Date:	Grid ref:	☀ ☁ ⛈

Hatch Notes

Water Temp:	Flow: L M H	Water Color: Clear Stained Muddy

Fish Caught

Trip Notes

Date:	Grid ref:	☼ ☁ ⛈

Hatch Notes

Water Temp:	Flow: L M H	Water Color: Clear Stained Muddy

Fish Caught

Trip Notes

Date:	Grid ref:	☀ ☁ ⛈

Hatch Notes

Water Temp:	Flow: L M H	Water Color: Clear Stained Muddy

Fish Caught

Trip Notes

Date:	Grid ref:	☀ ☁ ⛈

Hatch Notes

Water Temp:	Flow: L M H	Water Color: Clear Stained Muddy

Fish Caught

Trip Notes

Date:	Grid ref:	☀ ☁ ⛈

Hatch Notes

Water Temp:	Flow: L M H	Water Color: Clear Stained Muddy

Fish Caught

Trip Notes

Date:	Grid ref:	☀ ☁ ⛈

Hatch Notes

Water Temp:	Flow: L M H	Water Color: Clear Stained Muddy

Fish Caught

Trip Notes

Date:	Grid ref:	☀ ☁ ⛈

Hatch Notes

Water Temp:	Flow: L M H	Water Color: Clear Stained Muddy

Fish Caught

Trip Notes

Date:	Grid ref:	☀ ☁ ⛈

Hatch Notes

Water Temp:	Flow: L M H	Water Color: Clear Stained Muddy

Fish Caught

Trip Notes

Date:	Grid ref:	☀ ☁ ⛈

Hatch Notes

Water Temp:	Flow: L M H	Water Color: Clear Stained Muddy

Fish Caught

Trip Notes

Date:	Grid ref:	☀ ☁ ⛈

Hatch Notes

Water Temp:	Flow: L M H	Water Color: Clear Stained Muddy

Fish Caught

Trip Notes

Date:	Grid ref:	☀ ☁ ⛈

Hatch Notes

Water Temp:	Flow: L M H	Water Color: Clear Stained Muddy

Fish Caught

Trip Notes

Date:	Grid ref:	☼ ☁ ⛈

Hatch Notes

Water Temp:	Flow: L M H	Water Color: Clear Stained Muddy

Fish Caught

Trip Notes

Date:	Grid ref:	☀ ☁ ⛈

Hatch Notes

Water Temp:	Flow: L M H	Water Color: Clear Stained Muddy

Fish Caught

Trip Notes

Date:	Grid ref:	☀ ☁ ⛈

Hatch Notes

Water Temp:	Flow: L M H	Water Color: Clear Stained Muddy

Fish Caught

Trip Notes

Date:	Grid ref:	☀ ☁ ⛈

Hatch Notes

Water Temp:	Flow: L M H	Water Color: Clear Stained Muddy

Fish Caught

Trip Notes

Date:	Grid ref:	☼ ☁ ⛈

Hatch Notes

Water Temp:	Flow: L M H	Water Color: Clear Stained Muddy

Fish Caught

Trip Notes

Date:	Grid ref:	☀ ☁ ⛈

Hatch Notes

Water Temp:	Flow: L M H	Water Color: Clear Stained Muddy

Fish Caught

Trip Notes

Date:	Grid ref:	☀ ☁ ⛈

Hatch Notes

Water Temp:	Flow: L M H	Water Color: Clear Stained Muddy

Fish Caught

Trip Notes

Date:	Grid ref:	☀ ☁ ⛈

Hatch Notes

Water Temp:	Flow: L M H	Water Color: Clear Stained Muddy

Fish Caught

Trip Notes

Date:	Grid ref:	☼ ☁ ⛈

Hatch Notes

Water Temp:	Flow: L M H	Water Color: Clear Stained Muddy

Fish Caught

Trip Notes

Date:	Grid ref:	☀ ☁ ⛈

Hatch Notes

Water Temp:	Flow: L M H	Water Color: Clear Stained Muddy

Fish Caught

Trip Notes

Date:	Grid ref:	☀ ☁ ⛈

Hatch Notes

Water Temp:	Flow: L M H	Water Color: Clear Stained Muddy

Fish Caught

Trip Notes

Date:	Grid ref:	☀ ☁ ☁☂

Hatch Notes

Water Temp:	Flow: L M H	Water Color: Clear Stained Muddy

Fish Caught

Trip Notes

Date:	Grid ref:	☼ ☁ ⛈

Hatch Notes

Water Temp:	Flow: L M H	Water Color: Clear Stained Muddy

Fish Caught

Trip Notes

Date:	Grid ref:	☀ ☁ ⛈

Hatch Notes

Water Temp:	Flow: L M H	Water Color: Clear Stained Muddy

Fish Caught

Trip Notes

Date:	Grid ref:	☀ ☁ ⛈

Hatch Notes

Water Temp:	Flow: L M H	Water Color: Clear Stained Muddy

Fish Caught

Trip Notes

Date:	Grid ref:	☀ ☁ ⛈

Hatch Notes

Water Temp:	Flow: L M H	Water Color: Clear Stained Muddy

Fish Caught

Trip Notes

Date:	Grid ref:	☀ ☁ ⛈

Hatch Notes

Water Temp:	Flow: L M H	Water Color: Clear Stained Muddy

Fish Caught

Trip Notes

Date:	Grid ref:	☀ ☁ ⛈

Hatch Notes

Water Temp:	Flow: L M H	Water Color: Clear Stained Muddy

Fish Caught

Trip Notes

Date:	Grid ref:	☀ ☁ ⛈

Hatch Notes

Water Temp:	Flow: L M H	Water Color: Clear Stained Muddy

Fish Caught

Trip Notes

Date:	Grid ref:	☀ ☁ ⛈

Hatch Notes

Water Temp:	Flow: L M H	Water Color: Clear Stained Muddy

Fish Caught

Trip Notes

Date:	Grid ref:	☀ ☁ ⛈

Hatch Notes

Water Temp:	Flow: L M H	Water Color: Clear Stained Muddy

Fish Caught

Trip Notes

Date:	Grid ref:	☀ ☁ ⛈

Hatch Notes

Water Temp:	Flow: L M H	Water Color: Clear Stained Muddy

Fish Caught

Trip Notes

Date:	Grid ref:	☀ ☁ ⛈

Hatch Notes

Water Temp:	Flow: L M H	Water Color: Clear Stained Muddy

Fish Caught

Trip Notes

Date:	Grid ref:	☀ ☁ ⛈

Hatch Notes

Water Temp:	Flow: L M H	Water Color: Clear Stained Muddy

Fish Caught

Trip Notes

Date:	Grid ref:	☼ ☁ ⛈

Hatch Notes

Water Temp:	Flow: L M H	Water Color: Clear Stained Muddy

Fish Caught

Trip Notes

Date:	Grid ref:	☀ ☁ ⛈

Hatch Notes

Water Temp:	Flow: L M H	Water Color: Clear Stained Muddy

Fish Caught

Trip Notes

Date:	Grid ref:	☀ ☁ ⛈

Hatch Notes

Water Temp:	Flow: L M H	Water Color: Clear Stained Muddy

Fish Caught

Trip Notes

Date:	Grid ref:	☀ ☁ ⛈

Hatch Notes

Water Temp:	Flow: L M H	Water Color: Clear Stained Muddy

Fish Caught

Trip Notes

Date:	Grid ref:	☀ ☁ ⛈

Hatch Notes

Water Temp:	Flow: L M H	Water Color: Clear Stained Muddy

Fish Caught

Trip Notes

Date:	Grid ref:	☀ ☁ ⛈

Hatch Notes

Water Temp:	Flow: L M H	Water Color: Clear Stained Muddy

Fish Caught

Trip Notes

Date:	Grid ref:	☀ ☁ ⛈

Hatch Notes

Water Temp:	Flow: L M H	Water Color: Clear Stained Muddy

Fish Caught

Trip Notes

Date:	Grid ref:	☀ ☁ ⛈

Hatch Notes

Water Temp:	Flow: L M H	Water Color: Clear Stained Muddy

Fish Caught

Trip Notes

Date:	Grid ref:	☀ ☁ ⛈

Hatch Notes

Water Temp:	Flow: L M H	Water Color: Clear Stained Muddy

Fish Caught

Trip Notes

Date:	Grid ref:	☀ ☁ ⛈

Hatch Notes

Water Temp:	Flow: L M H	Water Color: Clear Stained Muddy

Fish Caught

Trip Notes

Date:	Grid ref:	☀ ☁ ⛈

Hatch Notes

Water Temp:	Flow: L　　M　　H	Water Color: Clear　Stained　Muddy

Fish Caught

Trip Notes

Date:	Grid ref:	☀ ☁ ☁

Hatch Notes

Water Temp:	Flow: L M H	Water Color: Clear Stained Muddy

Fish Caught

Trip Notes

Date:	Grid ref:	☀ ☁ ⛈

Hatch Notes

Water Temp:	Flow: L M H	Water Color: Clear Stained Muddy

Fish Caught

Trip Notes

Date:	Grid ref:	☀ ☁ ⛈

Hatch Notes

Water Temp:	Flow: L M H	Water Color: Clear Stained Muddy

Fish Caught

Trip Notes

Date:	Grid ref:	☀ ☁ ⛈

Hatch Notes

Water Temp:	Flow: L M H	Water Color: Clear Stained Muddy

Fish Caught

Trip Notes

Date:	Grid ref:	☀ ☁ ⛈

Hatch Notes

Water Temp:	Flow: L M H	Water Color: Clear Stained Muddy

Fish Caught

Trip Notes

Printed in Great Britain
by Amazon